Transport Around the World

BOATS AND SHIPS

Chris Oxlade

Heinemann
LIBRARY

www.heinemann.co.uk
Visit our website to find out more information about Heinemann Library books.

To order:

 Phone 44 (0) 1865 888066

 Send a fax to 44 (0) 1865 314091

Visit the Heinemann Bookshop at www.heinemann.co.uk to browse our catalogue and order online.

First published in Great Britain by Heinemann Library,
Halley Court, Jordan Hill, Oxford OX2 8EJ,
a division of Reed Educational and Professional Publishing Ltd.

Heinemann is a registered trademark of Reed Educational and Professional Publishing Ltd.

OXFORD MELBOURNE AUCKLAND
JOHANNESBURG BLANTYRE GABORONE
IBADAN PORTSMOUTH (NH) USA CHICAGO

Designed by Paul Davies and Associates
Originated by Ambassador Litho ltd
Printed by South China Printing in Hong Kong/China

ISBN 0 431 13401 4 (hardback)   ISBN 0 431 13406 5 (paperback)
05 04 03 02 01   05 04 03 02 01
10 9 8 7 6 5 4 3 2 1   10 9 8 7 6 5 4 3 2 1

British Library Cataloguing in Publication Data

Oxlade, Chris
    Boats and ships. – (Transport around the world) (Take-off!)
    1.Ships – Juvenile literature 2.Boats and boating – Juvenile literature
    I.Title
    623.8'2

Acknowledgements

The publishers would like to thank the following for permission to reproduce photographs: Phil Thomas p8; Corbis: Neil Rabinowitz p5, Joel W Rogers p6, p9, Dave G Houser p14, p16, Carl Purcell pp19, 29; Quadrant Picture Library: Graham Laughton p4, Mike Nicholson p12, p20, p21; The Stock Market: Tom Stewart; Tony Stone Images: Gordon Fisher p10, Tony Craddock p11, David H Endersbee p17, Vince Streano p22, Sylvain Grandadam p23, John Lund p24, Ian Murphy p25, Oli Tennent p26, James Bareham p27, Robin Smith p28; Trip: H Rogers pp7, 18, M Garrett p15

Cover photograph reproduced with permission of Robert Harding.

Our thanks to Sue Graves and Hilda Reed for their advice and expertise in the preparation of this book.

Every effort has been made to contact copyright holders of any material reproduced in this book. Any omissions will be rectified in subsequent printings if notice is given to the publishers.

Contents

Any words appearing in the text in bold, **like this**, are explained in the Glossary.

What is a boat?

A boat is any small craft that floats on water. People use boats for fishing, for travelling and for fun. Ships are bigger than boats. They are mainly used for transport.

A sailing dinghy, which people use for fun.

sailing dinghy

The captain of a ship.

All ships have a **crew** of sailors. They **steer** the ship and work its machinery. The captain is the person in charge of the ship and its crew.

How boats work

This small boat is called a kayak. It is moved along with paddles.

Inuit people use kayaks when they go out to catch fish and seals. Their kayaks are long, thin boats covered in seal skin.

A paddler in a kayak.

paddles

paddler

kayak

rudder

propeller

The propeller and rudder of a large boat which help it move through the water.

Larger boats and ships have an **engine** that turns a **propeller**. The propeller pushes the boat through the water. A **rudder** steers the boat to the left or to the right.

Long boats and big ships

This wooden boat is called a long boat. People called Vikings built boats like this about a thousand years ago. Long boats had oars, and some had a square sail, too.

oars

A long boat like the ones Vikings built about a thousand years ago.

long boat

A Viking called Eric the Red is thought to have sailed all the way from Norway to Greenland in a long boat.

The steamship *Leviathan*, which carried passengers across the Atlantic Ocean.

This steamship was called *Leviathan*. Passengers travelled in it across the Atlantic Ocean between Europe and America.

The *Leviathan* was built about 150 years ago.

Where are boats used?

Ships and large boats travel from one port to another across the sea. They often have to sail through stormy weather and large waves.

A **cargo** ship, which carries goods across the sea.

cargo

Some boats do not go to sea. They only travel on rivers, lakes and **canals**. This wide, flat **barge** is carrying cargo along a river.

A barge carrying goods along a river.

Long ago, horses on paths along canals towed barges with a rope.

goods

barge

Fishing boats

Every day, fishermen go out to sea in their fishing boats to catch fish. Some fishing boats stay at sea for many days or even weeks.

Fishing boats go to sea in all weathers to bring fresh fish back to port.

A fishing boat.

fish

fishermen

Fishermen sorting out their catch.

Large nets are used to catch the fish. The fishermen throw the nets into the sea. The boat pulls them along behind it and traps the fish.

Gondolas

In Venice in Italy, there are **canals** instead of streets. People use boats called gondolas as taxis to get around the city.

prongs

gondola

The gondolas that people in Venice use to travel about the city.

At the **bow** of a gondola, there are six prongs sticking out. These prongs stand for the six parts into which Venice is divided.

pole   gondola   gondolier

A gondolier rowing his gondola.

The person who **rows** a gondola is called a
gondolier. The gondolier stands up and uses a
very long pole to **steer** and to move the
gondola forward

The gondolier twists the oar in the water so
that he doesn't have to lift it out as he rows.

15

Ferries

A ferry is a ship that carries cars, trucks, buses and passengers. The vehicles are parked on **decks** inside the ship. Passengers sit on the upper decks.

Large ferries have cafés, shops and sometimes even a cinema on board.

A ferry carrying passengers, cars and trucks across the sea.

upper decks

lower decks

B.C. FERRIES

SPIRIT OF VANCOUVER ISLAND

bow

ferry

door

cars

ramp

Cars driving down a
ramp to get off the ferry.

There is a huge door in the ferry's **bow**. It opens to
let vehicles drive on and off by a ramp. This type of
ferry is called a 'roll-on, roll-off' ferry.

Hydrofoils

passengers

hydrofoil

hull

Passengers boarding a hydrofoil.

A hydrofoil is a very fast type of boat. It is often used to carry passengers. Hydrofoils zoom along with their **hulls** out of the water.

Hydrofoils are only used for short journeys, because they are not safe in bad weather.

On the bottom of the hull are small wings called foils. As the hydrofoil speeds up, the foils lift it out of the water.

The foils lifting the hydrofoil out of the water as it gathers speed.

A hydrofoil can travel up to 100 km an hour.

hydrofoil

hull

foils

Aircraft carriers

An aircraft carrier is a type of ship used by a navy. It is like an airfield at sea. Planes can take off and land on its huge **deck**.

military planes

aircraft carrier

An aircraft carrier carrying **military** planes.

runway

An aircraft carrier has a runway along one of its sides.

plane

A strong wire stops the plane
when it lands on the deck.

A catapult gives planes a push so they can go fast
enough to take off. When the planes land, a strong
wire stretched across the deck stops them.

Sailing

A junk is a sailing ship used in China for moving **cargo**. When the wind blows, it pushes on the sails, making the junk move along.

A Chinese junk moving cargo.

sails

junk

cargo

cloth sail

mast

junk

A junk with its cloth sails.

The junk's sails are made of cloth. Bamboo poles sewn to the sails make them stiff. Sails are held up by tall, wooden masts.

Container ships

Containers are metal boxes that are filled with different sorts of goods or **cargo**. A container ship carries hundreds of containers in its **hold** and on its **deck**.

deck

A container ship with its cargo in metal containers.

containers

hold

crane

ship

containers

Huge cranes loading containers on to a ship.

Containers arrive at **ports** on lorries and goods trains. Huge cranes load the containers on to the ship.

The containers are always a size that will fit on ships, trains or lorries.

Power boats

Power boats skimming across the surface of the water.

A power boat is a small, fast boat used for racing. Power boats have very powerful **engines**.

There are two main types of power boat racing: racing at sea and **circuit** racing on lakes.

When the sea is rough, a power boat jumps from wave to wave. The **crew** have a very bumpy ride, so they must wear seat belts and crash helmets.

helmet

seat belt

A power boat with its crew.

The longest circuit race is the 24-hour race held in Rouen, France, every year.

Cruise liners

A cruise liner is a ship on which people spend their holidays. On the ship there are places to eat, shops, swimming pools and rooms called cabins for passengers.

A large cruise liner in a busy **dockyard**.

cruise liner

dock

ship

lifeboat

life jackets

People wearing life jackets in a lifeboat.

A cruise liner carries small boats called lifeboats.
If something goes wrong, the passengers and **crew**
climb into the lifeboats and are lowered safely into
the sea.

When the liner *Titanic* sank in 1912 after
hitting an iceberg, many people died because
there were not enough lifeboats for everyone.

29

Timeline

3500 BCE	The Ancient Egyptians build sailing ships with square sails and oars. They are the first sailing ships that we know about.
1000 CE	The Viking people of Northern Europe build strong wooden long boats. They make long journeys across the seas to fight and trade.
1519	The Portuguese explorer Ferdinand Magellan and crew set out from Europe. One of his ships sails completely around the world.
1620	Dutchman Cornelis Drebbel builds the world's first submarine. It is a rowing boat covered with leather to keep out the water.
1776	The first submarine used as a weapon was called the *Turtle*. During the American War of Independence, it tried to sink an English ship in New York harbour – but it failed.
1808	A boat called the *Clermont* carries passengers along rivers in the USA. It is the first boat powered by a steam **engine**.
1912	The passenger liner *Titanic* sinks after hitting an iceberg in the Atlantic Ocean. More than 1500 people lose their lives.
1959	The first hovercraft, invented by Christopher Cockerell, is tested. It is called the *SR-N1*.

Glossary

barge   a long flat boat

bow   front of a boat or ship

canal   deep, wide ditch filled with water that boats and ships can sail along

cargo   goods carried on a ship

circuit   in a circle, going around and back to the beginning

crew   people who work on the boat or ship

deck   floor on the top of or inside a boat

dockyard   place where ships are loaded, unloaded and mended

engine   machine that uses fuel to move something. A ship's engine moves the ship along.

hold   part of a ship where cargo is stored

hull   main part of a boat or ship. The hull sits in the water.

military   used by people in armies or navies

port   place on the coast or on a large river where ships go to load and unload their cargo

propeller   the part of a boat that spins round and moves the boat forward

row   move and steer a boat using oars or long pole

rudder   the part of the boat that is used to steer

steer   guide the direction of the boat or ship

stern   back of a boat or ship

Index

Titles in the *Transport Around the World* series include:

Hardback   0 431 13 402 2

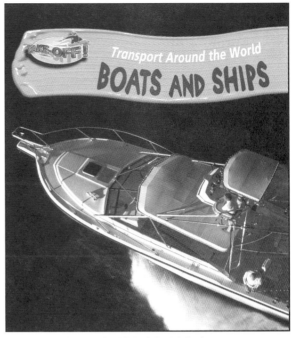

Hardback   0 431 13 401 4

Hardback   0 431 13 403 0

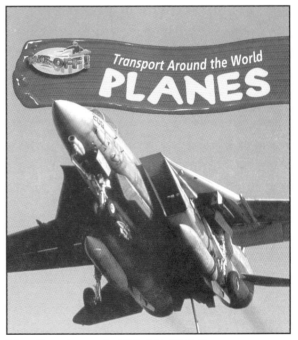

Hardback   0 431 13 400 6

Find out about the other titles in this series on our website www.heinemann.co.uk/library